I Cry Unto You, O Lord

I Cry Unto You, O Lord

poems of lament

by

SARAH SUZANNE NOBLE

CLADACH
Publishing

I Cry unto You, O Lord: Poems of Lament
© 2019 by Sarah Suzanne Noble
All rights reserved.
Art and Photography by Sarah Suzanne Noble

An AGATES Book of Poetry

Published by
Cladach Publishing
Greeley, CO 80633
http://cladach.com

All scripture quotations are taken from the Holy Bible, New International Version, NIV. Copyright 1973, 1978, 1984, by International Bible Society. Used by permission of Zondervan Publishing House. All rights reserved.

ISBN: 9781945099175
Library of Congress Control Number: 2019943806
Printed in the United States of America

*We are all restless
till we find our rest in Thee.*

–SAINT AUGUSTINE

Special Thanks

to

my husband, Jonny.

&

both my mother and my mother-in-law
for their constant encouragement.

&

Park Community Church Chicago
for loving me while in the fire—especially
Pastor Jackson Crum, Bill and Mindy Meier,
and the Payne family for their support
of my family and of me as a writer.

TABLE OF CONTENTS

Introduction 11

I. PAIN 15

Suffering 17
Sunrise 20
Tears of Dew 21
Waiting 22
Words 25
Window 26
Act 27
Bare Feet 29
Stiff Neck 30
Wells 31
Heavy 32
Quilt 34
Bray 35
Crush 37
White Flag 38
Change 40
Pin 41
Inch of Snow 43
Steel 44
To Prepare 45
Wail 46
Migraine 49
Greenhouse 50
Menthol 51
Splinter 52

Web 54
Clay Jar 57
Restless 58
Illness 59
Disappointment 60
This too Shall Pass 62
Light 63

II. BEAUTY 65

Palm 67
Sky 68
Song 69
Dreams 71
Moon 72
Star 73
Daffodil 74
Children 75
Walk 76
Tiles of Beauty 78
Puddles 81
Ice 82
Trees Clap 83
Layers 84
Gallery 86
Snowflakes 87
Painting of White 89
Hunt 90
Stained Glass 92
Bubbling Brook 94

III. CHRIST 97

Sight 99
Hear 100

Taste 101
Scent 102
Touch 104
Fall 106
Weight of Glory 108
Gift 109
Sabbatical Break 110
Remember 112
Focus 113
Preparation 114
Holy One 116
Right Now 118
King 119
Mercy 121
Bow 122
To Be a Baby 124
Fix My Eyes 125
Sacrifice 126

IV. WONDER 129

Captured 131
Fully Known 132
Heaven's Gate 133
When the Moon Rises 134
Breakthrough 135
Rose and Thorn 136
Humbled 138
Seedling 139

About the Poet 141

INTRODUCTION

I am a mother of two small children, the wife of a hard working husband, and daughter of our faithful Father. I have undergone two back surgeries in the past five years, recovered from PPD, wrestled with insomnia, and recovered from concussions and other injuries. I write, paint, plant and do whatever I can to seek the Lord's face and cultivate beauty in this season of suffering.

My writings, sketches, and photos represent a portion of my work in this past year. Countless paintings have been sent to dear friends who are in the trenches so to speak. My hope is that these poems will provide language to others who suffer and, as in David's beautiful psalms, a format that expresses honesty and glory to our heavenly Father.

My process is one "in process." I typically write in the midst of pain or waiting, with metaphors that lead me to Christ. As I write, my vision widens and I remember the scripture of my youth, the truth of who God is; He is my mighty sovereign Savior.

The work is divided into four categories: Pain, Beauty, Christ, and Wonder. These tend to be the focus of the majority of the poems. They cover nearly the whole spectrum of admiration, praise, confession and supplication, as well as lament. Intermingled are scriptures, art, and photos I have taken in various places in Illinois and Indiana, and art I have sketched or painted. The scriptures listed served as an anchor, and the beauty of the photos as wind in my sails—truly a daily blessing. The intent is that the collection breathes worship and comforts hearts.

Perhaps this book could be a gift to someone you know who is in the trenches looking for light, a tool that can be used to sift for truth.

> *The Lord bless you and keep you;*
> *the Lord make his face shine on you*
> *and be gracious to you;*
> *the Lord turn his face toward you*
> *and give you peace.*
>
> —Numbers 6:24-26

Sarah Suzanne Noble
Chicago, Illinois

PAIN

Save me, O God,
for the waters have come up to my neck.
I sink in the miry depths,
where there is no foothold.
I have come into the deep waters;
the floods engulf me.
I am worn out calling for help;
my throat is parched.
My eyes fail,
looking for my God.

–Psalm 69:1-4

SUFFERING

Surrounded by frozen vegetables,
   burritos, gel pads, freezer packs,
   these things mountains
   and my weak, inflamed body the valley.

I cry out to you, Lord. No answer.
   When will this suffering stop?
   Like a caterpillar I grovel on the ground;
   could this be my rest?

A cocoon, transformation
   from this lowly body;
   in this life healing, joy, change?
   Will I float from lightness?

Will I be bright as a flower,
   ornamented as my wedding day?
   So many questions, no answers;
   I am not in control, nor do I understand.

This I know: you are a good Father
   who works in all things for my good.
   You will replace mourning with laughter,
   sackcloth with a robe.

I do so feel it has been the year of burlap;
   pain upon strain, toil, tears in soil,
   hope, pain, hope: a cycle of suffering,
   months of mockery in my head.

Savior, please break this rhythm of my life,
    be the source of new waves.
    As a pebble drops in a pond,
    dear Rock of Ages, crash in the water.

Would there be a new and beautiful flow,
    pattern, sight coming from thee
    with shouts of praise, screams of delight?—
    Lord, please, a break from the fight.

Would there be jubilation, merriment, joy,
    laughter, delight, gaiety and might,
    rest ushered in this year, a sabbatical break,
    a time of community and communion.

Father, restore Sarah Noble,
    restore Mr. Noble, till they praise you
    with laughs and leap like youthful deer,
    and tell your deeds to the next generation.

How do they praise you
    when suffering is all they've seen?
    Would an avalanche of your mercy
    pour down into this sunken valley?

Raise my plain to a plateau then a peak
    that I may peek on the face of the I Am,
    as I become still, no fire of pain,
    the Eternal Flame revealed.

How I long for relief in your presence,
    for the weak made strong,

to dine at your table of delights,
to walk with you in light.

To laugh, to wave palms, to rest
under your canopy; heal, sustain,
give daily bread. By your goodness
raise high this woman laid low.

SUNRISE

Will the sun rise?
Will this pain flee?
Twilights obscure, dust refracts, my spirit lacks.
In between night and morning,
    in between earth and heaven,
    mercy, dear Father, mercy!
I bow before your throne of grace.
Bring healing to this place!
Remove the pain,
    strands no longer sting,
    eyes no longer wet,
    bones straight, discs hydrate,
    paths of pain removed from brain,
    ache acute dulled:
    be gone by our Savior's blood.
Loosen my muscles, relieve the migraines.
Tension turns limp, shakes subside.
Come to your throne with confidence
    I lack most times.
By Jesus' name and blood infuse me with life.
Help my unbelief, help!
Jacob wrestled for the night;
    then blessing, favor, grace,
    protection in this place.
Help me to learn obedience in this season.
Remind me of your love.
Set my heart on things above.
May I find peace and rest?
I think the sun is rising.

TEARS OF DEW

Drip, drop, drip, drop
   salt water to the earth;
   how will seeds grow from tears?
How does mourning cease?
   Each morning and each night
   dew drops on my pillow.
Paths of pain run down my face.

Is there another way, oh Lord?
   Downpours of healing;
   My body (mentally) kneeling.
Fortified faith, forgiving family.

Eyes peering through rain,
   not the sting of salt on skin,
   a fight for my body weighed down.
My eyes stare at cracks in the ceiling.

Waiting, Lord, waiting for healing,
   saltwater waves fill most of the earth.
   Please let me taste the fruit
from flowing rivers, bubbling brooks.

Water from melons, drops from clouds,
   divine appeal before evening meal,
   sprouts protected from freeze.
Blossoms blow in the breeze.

WAITING

Knots, knobs, molting bark, a metaphor for back;
twisted branches, vertebrae, awkward promenade.
The roots deep, dusty; hardships endured, trials, heat.
How lovely is the sycamore bark?
Watch it shed, peel to reveal brown, green, gold.
It grows most grand, by your hand watered, and it works.
It takes our breath and returns it as life.

Father you take our stench and make miraculous myrtle;
our sweat, pressed wine; our wrinkles, smiles.
Though we bathe, pungent aromas waft and rise.
Thank you for making us white in your sight.
Inclusive of the full range of color,
through your prism we shine, source of visible light.
No darkness in you, but sapphires, garnets, opal bright.
The wind rises, surrounds me, reminds of the unseen.
As the true Gardener, please plant us in sun
where water is flowing and fields dance.
Be the fence post that supports us, Lord.
Help us to rise to the harvest, to bear fruit in time,
accept the pruning process and yield the wine.
Tie me to you, rope me to rods, staple me to sticks.
Praise you, Father, barbed wire isn't my cup,
only the True Vine wrapped it, that last supper,
Christ's hands and feet nailed to a tree for all to see,
blood dripping, falling onto the dirt,
the same dirt from which we're formed, fed.
The Father breathed life; the Son breathed his last.
Like the sycamore tree, you turn our breath to life again.
You supply needs of the weary and sap for the tree.

WORDS

Confined to my head, no more painting,
    words make pictures in this season of waiting.
The chill wind, cold again;
    at least it's not pain, but a friend.

Lord, you are the God who sees,
    who by grace meets all our needs.
It's hard for me even to bow
    or raise arms high; please deliver now!

May the numbness, burning and ache
    subside, give a long-needed break.
Would thoughts not be interrupted by pain,
    new paths of joy forged in my brain?

The clock ticks, tocks, our boat rocks;
    do you sleep in this storm, dear One?
I of little faith at these times
    lament, plead in stories and rhymes.

Lord, thanks for the good in the difficult and bad,
    the spiritual fruits we now have;
the feast of friendship, sincere smiles,
    loved ones beside us in trials.

Provision and protection from your hand:
    home, clothes, shelter in our native land;
fingers to type, tears of reflection,
    broken mirrors of introspection.

WINDOW

Window tall and square, I lie and stare:
  buds, leaves, brown falling;
  heat, ice, heat, ice, aching;
  some relief, then burning again,
  twigs in the wind, kindling for fire;
  clouds of grey, dark night coming;
  turmeric's pungent, earthy taste;
  vinegar, sour on a sponge.
Magnolias will come, I know it;
  pink blooms, petaled sidewalks.
Thirty three my age; arthritis my disease;
  my daughter merry, running;
  redbud leaves gone, hearts droop,
  holly berries red wonders.
Thirty-three years Jesus lived;
  agony, then Easter morn.
Daffodils fresh, green, poking,
  tulips bowing, Hyacinths sweet
  know when to celebrate.
My son will return; Christ returned,
  the pain removed, victory secure.
  Body braces removed, healing proved.
No more waiting.
Rocks rolled away; what of dismay?—
  forgotten in the celebration;
  dancing, limbo, lingering laugh—
  glimpse of the future, perhaps.

ACT

Father. please restore;
   ensure your servant's life.
Father, please heal;
   your word is a surgeon's knife.

Father, please protect
   my mind, heart, soul, body.
Father, please redeem
   my past, present, future.

Father, please uphold
   with your loving hands.
Father, please speak,
   your Word, illuminating lamp.

Father, please guard
   from lies, worries, stumbling feet.
Father, please act;
   comfort, raise, majestic King.

Father, please act;
   end this suffering trial.
Father, please act;
   turn sorrows to smiles.

Do something, Lord;
   remedy, reclaim.
Help me take steps forward
   in your powerful name.

BARE FEET

Burning back, sweat-soaked sheets,
   painful day; then repeat.
Children scream, now smile;
   parenting is worthwhile.
Each morning's sun brings mercy.
Daring to hope, braces become beautiful.
Ice to quench fire; time will restore.

Moments of childhood delight:
   bare feet on November day;
   pink-striped, purple-streaked,
   blue-covered night,
   silhouettes in sight;
   slobbery kisses, soft blankets,
   coffee shared, release of cares.

Release control; it was never mine
   but an illusion, something hurtful, sad.
Toes tingle, my request mingles with
   hopes of leaping and joyful reaching.

Fingers rise, light filters.
Warmth on my skin, not a burn.
Arms extended, back expanded,
   weightless flow
   of healing glory.
Lips laced with smiles, food in piles,
   fellowship with the Father,
   barefoot walk in the garden.
Restoration and reconciliation.

STIFF NECK

Sour attitude
Pain like perfume
Restless roars
Does God snore?
Dark, fear, pain
No spoil or gain
Warrior entrenched
Awful stench
Deserted, tired
Under fire
Soul above
Soaring dove
Olive branch
Another chance
Pilot steers
In the clear
Wings gliding
Sails flying
Victory, conquest
Triumph, success
Beautiful bride
Savior on high
Holy Spirit within
Freedom from sin
Redirect, resurrect
Redeem stiff necked.

WELLS

My eyes are wells, my cheeks swell.
Again at this place: pillow over my face.
Frustrating pain, fleeting patience.
Lord, restore my lot again.
Please forgive for sins unchanged.
Hold me, Father, when I slip.
Things appear dark, and I trip.
Scoop me as only a dear father can.

Hold me in strong arms that understand.
Cradle me, caress me, wipe away tears.
I'm still your child at thirty-three years.
Rock me, soothe me, sing me a song.
Sing of Love so high, deep and long.
Rest my head in peace through the night.
I almost feel my eyelids brush your face
as You gently lay me down in place.

In the morning, let light surge in,
cascading over walls, flooding halls.
I rise from bed; you lift me up.
With a smile, you hand me a cup.
I drink the offerings I did not earn.
No longer do eyes and cheeks burn.
You toss me high, as high as you can.
I know what hope feels like, soaring again.

HEAVY

Fingertips heavy with the ink they must write.
Dripping droplets in the middle of the night.
Prayers for dear friends far and near.
For recovery, faith, work and tears.
For restoration—more than we imagine.
For reconciliation, hearts to gladden.

Eyes heavy, dry; formation of a stye.
Inflammation; my voice sighs.
Swollen marshmallow puffs underground.
Heal me, Lord; and heal others.

Equip my sisters and brothers.
Give them a helmet to guard from the torrent.
Direct our hearts toward beauty and praise.
Shield our faith when arrows are raised.
Let us strike the accuser with your word.
Let truth reign and fit us well.
Ready our feet for peace to tell.

Would this armor be unfashionably light,
weigh like a feather, but guard us at night.
Would your scales remove the weight,
the heavy pressure of our bodies that fail.
May our bodies become balloons filled
with your breath, expanded to rise in you.

QUILT

Grey sticks twist, bend and peak;
   green bud unfolds like a flower.
Star of hope in mid November;
   will snowflakes fill the sky, I wonder?
That same bark is wrapped with lights
   glowing in the winter nights.
Patchwork quilts covering toes,
   crackling fire logs warm our nose.
I think my back is a quilt, covered
   with scars, stitches, and surgeons' wishes.

Are quilts a thing of necessity or beauty,
   each one pointing to its maker?
Hemmed in, cross stitched with careful craft,
   melody of colors, promise of warmth.
Are veils a thing of beauty or necessity,
   shielding prominence and glory?
Translucent or opaque pure linen—
   white, blue, purple and scarlet;
Separation to beauty, by beauty,
   temporary, permanent rainbow promise.
The curtain tore as Christ breathed his last,
   no vapor was spotted, only death.

Jesus the Lamb championed eternity,
   Christ child wrapped in swaddling clothes
Now wrapped in linen burial swaths;
   he left them in the rock, arose.
Later he ascended with his cloak ablaze.
   Now, toward heaven we yearn.

BRAY

As the donkey tail sways, his voice hee-haws,
   my vision wanders in the fog,
   his bray, like mine, raspy and worn.

Of all things, a pill stuck and tore my throat,
   and I feared shame and embarrassment;
   neither he nor I want grief before we die.

Grief and the grave you gracefully bore;
   though you abhor our sin-muddy deceit,
   you draw close in the midst of suffering.

I want your hand holding me, or else nothing;
   your palm etched with my name
   and others you'll never forget.

Guide me on, my beacon of light,
   exposing waves, rocks and plight,
   predicament, quandary, dire straits.

From the lion that roars and devours bait
   to swaying grass by still, clear waters,
   to butterflies mingling,
   to sons and daughters,
   to bunches of grapes, juicy and sweet,
   to honey dripping like pomegranate seeds,
   to bounty and beauty,
   to things restored,
   to a donkey that sings and hee-haws no more.

CRUSH

Body crushed
Spirit withers
Always winter
Tears pour
Heart freezes
Help, Jesus!
Melt anger
Shape my soul
Restore the old

Salt sears
Blood smears
Living sacrifice
Holy sacrament
Life through another
His strong power
Imparted every hour
Look we elsewhere
No way to compare
To his promises
In his word

He sees you now
Faithful servant
Continue on
He will guide
Keep from harm
Lead, revive

WHITE FLAG

My core wrestles
   like a child tugging
   tumbling, seething
Flag is raised
   surrenders knot
   anchors the sailing white
Whimpers from the wounded
   scars from the searing

Why is surrender white?
Why are flags raised high
   when one feels in the muck
   and darkness veils the eyes?

White like clouds, white like glory
   white like a new-unwritten story
A page in a book that yields to wind
   a song that's sung by a beckoning
Tossed, tattered, trailing
Loose, limp, laying
Shift, swift, lift
Soar, shine, star
Beacon brimming

  Forgiveness for sinning
  Victory in defeat
  Christ washes our feet
  First I raise my flag
    let the Father decide
  Tackle the wind

Yield to the storm
Rest in the sun
Stiff in the cold
Made alive again

Submission, tied to pole
Raised high for all to see
   the struggle, toil, victory
Heart rest in righteousness
   not of my own; of his throne
Mind relents to silent
   peace from our True Home.
Soul yearns for truth and beauty
   seeking first his kingdom come
Body waiting through the groans
   to rejoice at new Heaven and Earth

Wave valiantly, banner, till you retire
Hems will break, threads will tear
   then lowered to the ground
   with ceremonious sound
Trumpet Taps, then tunes triumphant
The flag is folded, encased in glass
   crowned with honor and glory
A beat-up flag points to our story
   to Christ immortal, interceding
   listening, oh, listening to our pleading
The great High Priest knows the drill
He himself was raised and spilled
For a plethora of saints past, present
   proclaiming the victory won
A white flag of triumph ever waves

CHANGE

I stare at glass,
  moisture on door.
The air has changed,
  cold nose, cold floor.
Temperature change
  allows me to see
what has always been
  and what will be.
Hydrogen, nitrogen
  oxygen absorbs.
Dew drops form
  through the night.
A change, a display
  an act of insight.
Could it be we see
  the Holy Spirit work
when circumstances or
  transitions occur?
A trace is left for us
  to confirm and assure
That he's been there.
  All along, we dwell secure.
God's indwelling Spirit
  mysterious and light
sees me as a temple
  to house his might.
Whispers are heard
  when wind meets grass.
I think my Savior passed.

PIN

Pin pricks back
Pain is back
No strings, just holes
Knots swollen
Mend me, Lord
Mend my heart
Heal that as a start
Stitch, sew, needlepoint
Patch the doubt
Hem my faith
Press my heart
Pattern my mind
Put pain behind
Soothe my sorrow
Remind of tomorrow
Where mercies spring
Where bows are tied
Where you are glorified

Thank you
For knowing pain
Of nails, not pins
For holes in hands
Spears in your side
For taking my pride
For seeing, saving
Each and every tear

INCH OF SNOW

An inch of snow
April groans
Crocus covered
Daffodils droop
Birds nest
Children rest
Indoors we wait
Springtime promised
Comes again
By God's grace
Expectant waiting
Beauty revealed
New life displayed
We wait with gratitude
For warm house
Children and spouse
Our Savior's return
A promise assured
A Priest understood
We wait...
Lord, help me wait

STEEL

Nerves of steel now molting
Fire's flame was scorching
Smoke in nostrils, wheezy coughing
Eyes burning, fire on the lamp
My daughter's blanket lit
Pick it up with bare hands
It spreads, it drops, it treads
My son watches from the sofa
With a blanket I smother,
With my body, snuff out the flame
Carpet burnt, alarms sound
Babies cry

Old windows, cool breeze
Fresh oxygen to breathe
Hold my son, hold my daughter
Thank you, Lord, we're safe inside
Thank you, little ones sigh
Thank you the fire was caught
Puzzle pieces, toys and table
All escaped the blaze

I'm amazed at the timing
To wait on naps
To smell the smoke stack
To contact neighbors and husband
To exchange tears with hugs
To replace two carpet squares
Toss wedding blanket on the floor
Mercies new each morning, each hour

TO PREPARE

Conditioning my soul
Preparing my mind
   to look ahead
   to forget what's behind
I see the pattern now
It took me so long
   to recognize recovery
   to sing a new song
Setback, despair, pain
   grips, seeps, shocks
   when the surprise settles
   satan knocks
Lock the door
Reach out for help
   to praying friends
My being melts
   weeping, wailing
   resting, releasing
Turn on music
   familiar worship
   song by song
My courage rises
   to come to you
   to write
   let you dry my eyes
I seek your face
   ask bold prayers
   lie silently
   llisten in layers
   to soft-spoken words
I recline, receive

WAIL

A prolonged, high-pitched cry
  of pain, grief, or anger
Wail, I wail
  again at this place
I know it well:
  salt on face
  mascara smeared
Quick to recall
  the past year's yowls
  the howls, moans, groans
  the pain in the dark

Yet, Lord, you lift sore necks
You bring to mind victories:
  valiant saints, genuine friends
  prayer-filled halls
  cancers cured
  fertility given
  those led to the grave
  gripped, saved
  spouses reconciled
  rest for a little while

Train my mind to remember
  Spring is coming
Light is gaining
Praise you, Lord
Soul, sing!
Sing of grace, of glory
Sing of the unchanging story!

MIGRAINE

Migraine tightens
Eyes squint in pain
Baby sleeps
So much to do

You call me to rest
Know you are God
My mind tries to race
I can't slow the pace

Thank you for quiet
A calm in the chill
For quilts to cover
To comfort the ache

Grayness and silence
One brings the other
Help me to embrace it
Like infant to mother

Muscles refreshed
Strength restored
I depend on you
I rely on your Word

Carry me close
Covered, calm
Breathing deeply
At rest in your arms

GREENHOUSE

Powder white
Feathery soft
Specks of dirt
No dots of depletion

Bugs invade, hide
Lay eggs at night
Spreading, breeding
Covered while reading
Infestation insult
Fear, worry, destruction

Toss it all, tear it up
Look away, tears build up
Like manna that rots
We can't cling to flowers
Can't hold on to spring

But …

Thank you for the sunshine
For breaks at rest time
For prayers and coffee
For quiet in the cacophony

All is good; thank you, Lord
Help me continue to plant
Broadcast seeds in fertile soil
Then delight in you
As I watch them unfurl

MENTHOL

Menthol perfume
  both icy and hot
  burns yet brings relief

Signals change
  myrrh resin
  produced from thorns
  for aches and sprains

Frankincense grows on rock
  slashed then seeps
  collected for perfume
  gifts for a king

Production similar
  flesh and tree
  thorny crown
  Savior seeps

The presents bestowed
  at great cost
  our gift revealed
  on the cross

SPLINTER

My back aches
Daily I stretch
Daily I pray
Slow progress
Eventually points of strength

Is now the time
To stop stretching?
I may feel good
For a week or two
But pain returns
Like a mouse
Unwelcome, creeping
It sneaks in

Muscles tense, body aches
Break in discipline, huge mistake

Our spiritual life is war also
We read, we recover
We have fresh sight
Then we try walking
The day turns to night
We need your light
To strive toward you

Daily we need you
Daily we come
Lord, give us endurance
Help us resist deceit

In delight and freshness
Help us start our days
With eyes clear and voices raised
Minds guarded from satan's lie—
The 'Oh, I am fine'

There is never a
Time that I am fine
Apart from you
I wither, I die
My muscles weaken
My body sighs
Tendons tighten
Anger enters
Splinters fester

Give strength for today
Sight through morning fog
Light my way.

WEB

My body is made of spider webs—
    delicate, fine, ripped and blown;
    muscles made of tinsel tone,
    shredded, lost and filled with moss—

Slow and weak, stiff and meek.
    But every day the master mends,
    beautifully weaving, carefully crafting,
    rebuilding this structure for another day.

Arise and see the drops of dew
    sparkling there across the spin.
    My ragged web I could not sew, but
    mercy from God has come unseen.

As spiders spin and work each day
    God is working in my dismay—
    improbable the task, yet every eve
    creating a beautiful, fragile display.

CLAY JAR

My clay cracks; this jar so worn,
   broken, holds no more.
How could treasure be tucked inside?
   I just want to hide.
How can something that's so brilliant
   rest here in my dust?
Freely it seeps through all my cracks
   the way his glory must.

Armor of God, hold your ground,
   let majesty resound.
Potter, mend me for tasks at hand,
   and give me strength to stand.
Please glaze over my imperfections,
   my heathen introspections,
sinner's sorrow, flock's fears.
   Please remove the tears.

Out of my dust form a vessel
   of worth while I wrestle.
Guard the treasure deep inside.
   In my weakness, be my strength.
'God is with us,' may I proclaim!
   He is near, I'm chosen.
Song of my heart, sonnet of my speech,
   Jesus Christ may I preach!
Though scoffers scoff at what's unseen,
   may I rest in thee.

Repentance leads to rivers, acceptance to accolades.
Truth turns to triumph, and clay to jars.

RESTLESS

Pounding heart a raging sea,
    thoughts race effortlessly.
Breath short, head tight,
    something about the long night.
The darkest day of the year is near.

I long for days with yellow tones,
    for bare toes on cool, green grass.
I long for birdsong, fluttering flowers,
    for things soaring, high and upward.
Awake my soul; awake and cheer.

In darkness see brilliant stars above,
    see Boy below as long foretold.
Hark, it's a miracle manifest—
    reconciled, loved, all forgiven.
Child of God, life is worth living!

Brighter than starlight, grander than angel song,
    deeper than ocean roar, higher than eagle soar.
Mightier than death, creator of breath,
    Jesus Christ, Spirit of peace.
He brings victory, conquest, release.

ILLNESS

Father, I pray for aches to subside;
   let me witness you on high.
Clouds part, glory shines;
   thank you, Lord, that you are mine.

When pain penetrates and fever persists
   my mind is carried up toward your bliss.
I see colors: emeralds green,
   golden bracelets and jeweled crowns.

As I ponder, remember my Lord,
   mercy and faithfulness fall on me.
Fluttering in breeze, pooled in eddies,
   I see your bounty, feel your grace.

Beautiful Savior in the grass,
   talking to the sheep that pass;
I see a King now robed in red
   as I lie awake, here in my bed.

Weeping willows wane no more
   dancing by the edge of shore.
Geese in flocks, meander and dwell
   in warm places laden with shells.

I see a Father holding me,
   rocking me gently upon his knee.
I hear him whisper in my ear,
   'Daughter, this is temporary; have no fear.'

A cup of water I take to sleep.
My Lord will deliver me.

DISAPPOINTMENT

Dreams, hopes, merriment mingle
Expectation's joyful tingle
But easy dreams are scorched by sun
Desires turn to wrath and scorn

Accusations linger, a burning loop
Caught in muck of a sorrow soup
Stuck in my own stubbornness
Seeking freedom from this mess

I turn to stone, don't want to feel
Emotions of dismay only too real
Hardened, cold I have become
Lured by the evil one

Father break the shackles of pity
I want to have joy in this city
Help me surrender my day, my life
Yield my all to the Bread of Life

Mix in me the yeast that rises
The joy of submission that surprises
To vex no more, to just be light
I need to forgive and not to fight

Take my hands, release my grip
Lift my eyes so I don't trip
Your hands have holes, sores and scabs
Mine are softly strained and sad

Forgive me for unholy plans
For anger, laziness, and demands
For not turning to you sooner
For being a wax-and-wane lunar

Grief cannot compare with the cross
Rejection of a Son for the lost
For the wayward and the sojourner
For the grumbling, fitful sinner

Who confesses their sin and repents
Rock-carved grave can soften laments
The stone rolled away now offers
True joy, true happy-ever-after

Disappointment has no traction
With the delight of resurrection
Christ's victory dance, on dirt paths
His feast with friends who sorely lacked

His glory dimmed for moments bleak
Yet burns throughout eternity
Oh that my eyes would see Christ's plea
Offering the life he gave for me

THIS TOO SHALL PASS

This too will pass
Satan has no grasp
Redeemer grips my hand
Leads me on, I will stand

Wrestle of rest, body squirms
Spot on the sidewalk, a pink worm
Sun is hot, ground is warm
Birds circle, threat of harm

Creeping towards the promised land
Ground that's firm, not sinking sand
Time stands still, the sun stays high
Vultures cloud the heated sky

War is the sight inside of me
But you whisper songs of stillness
I hear your call to quietness
To trust in your strength and faithfulness

Inch forward or wait for my Rescuer?
His promises are sure, as I creep and stir
Someday I'll enter my promised rest
While I am here, Lord, help me stay

Do not delay as I pause midday
May I remain, may I abide
As I nestle into your pierced side

LIGHT

The light I delighted in,
   now hurts my head.
What once was joy,
   gives pain instead.
Blanket soft
   covers my eyes.
Breathe in deep,
   heavy sighs.
Sustainer of life,
   feed me once more.
Refresh me with waters
   on your peaceful shore.
Feed me your bread,
   my Passover Lamb.
You're the Alpha, Omega,
   the great I Am.
Revive my mind,
   restore my flesh.
I linger in your glory,
   bright Light in my chest.

BEAUTY

The heavens declare the glory of God;
the skies proclaim the work of his hands.
Day after day they pour forth speech;
night after night they reveal knowledge.

–Psalm 19:1-2

I remain confident of this:
I will see the goodness of the Lord
in the land of the living.
Wait for the Lord;
be strong and take heart
and wait for the Lord.

–Psalm 27:13-14

PALM

Palm branch, victory, triumph—
Raise shouts of adoration and praise
Our King enters on a foal
Humble processional
Step, trot toward the cross
Fronds wave victorious
Fanned then crushed under foot
The stump of Jesse, the holy shoot
Hosannas hard to hear
In this world he loves dear
The cost, the cost
The crucifixion
A scale so heavy
Heaping horrors leeching
Gone, vanquished, not recalled
Forgiven
A Son risen for all
Rest we now in the Father's hand
A palm so big, an outstretched fan
He cradles us in feathers of green
Shades us from things unseen
A sign of success, a wing of rampart
The failings of flesh, a repentant start

SKY

I stare at the sky
Watching clouds pass by
Some white, some grey
Some slow, some fly
Thin and wispy
Trailing blissfully
Blue backdrop
Pink burst
Low fog
Bleak smog
Time still
No frills

Then a new day
Fresh mercies
Sunrise
Changes in the sky
Remind of things high
Faith, hope, love
Creator above
Sustain and filter
Confetti's glitter
Doorway to deity
Prayerful piety

SONG

Chirping robins have not left,
    nestled in for winter rest;
home of berries, bark assortment,
    happy hybrid home apartment.

Neighbors to acorn piles,
    squatter on pine smiles;
plump from thanksgiving,
    plumes ample, no shivering.

Bright beak, carrot on the snowman,
    nests weaved like wreaths,
overflowing fountains, celebration
    songs all winter long.

Chimes keep cheerfully chirping,
    delight in day, in life;
songs in all seasons, regardless of flight
    toward the brilliant blue sky.

Perspective of thy beauty, revived
    liveliness, vitality and zest,
beauty adorned in a moment of rest;
    glide, descend with heavy sun.

To provision given by God's only Son,
    repent, repeat, enjoy the feast;
the bread, the body,
    the bounteous eternal relief.

DREAMS

    Joseph dreamed sheaves of grain.
       They all strain down, but cannot see.
    Moons and stars circle round,
       fall before him at the ground.

    A well of sorrow, a pit of disdain,
       lost to Egypt; his death they proclaim.
    Servanthood, sufferings; is this a dream?
       Will I wake from what I have seen?

    Is my name not Joseph, son of Israel—
       loved child, born of Rachel?
    Robe ripped, artwork unweave;
       seems so hard to believe.

    Yet dreams from God, through God, for God
       bind themselves, kneed and plod;
    time, patience, seasons pass,
       forward looking, raised mast.

    Loving fathers do not forget
       theirs sons, daughters, the yet.
    Stories turn true; a family reglued,
       an artist's insight, a father's delight,
    Nations restored, promises kept,
       joy proclaimed from those who wept.

MOON

We can stare at the moon, but not at the sun.
    Ray reflections run.
They caress the surface, they help us to see
    something we would know, not be.
The imperfections are visible:
    canyons, craters, chasms,
    gullies impossible to fathom.

What we see is but a trace of the glory
    and brilliance of the original face.
Lord, you see my imperfections.
    Someday I, too, will glow from confession.
Holy, holy, holy are you the righteous one.
    Cherubim and seraphim, come.
    At your command all was made.

The foundation of earth and moon were laid
    by your self-sustaining power;
The earth is bathed in light every hour,
    balance of all scientific might.
Heat expands, space contracts,
    a majestic, creative act.
    By you and in you all things are clear.

The order of nature, the shape of a sphere,
    yet holy, holy, holy are you,
    invincible, everlasting, blazing sunlight.

STAR

Star atop our tree
Spotlight of nativity
Resembles the pitch black sky
The bleakness, but then the sign
For all to see, and no king overthrow
Placed in heaven's open window
Brilliant, bright, breathtaking sight
On that glorious, beautiful night
Emmanuel, God among us
In straw and hay dwelt
Canes of shepherd, shadows cast
Lows of sheep among the grass
Mother's promised joy
Father's baby boy
Songs of angels surround
Multitudes in Bethlehem town
The promised Messiah has arrived
Man's debt, a living sacrifice
Wise men travel from the East
Gifts draped across their beasts
Star, star, brilliantly beaming
Spotlight of nativity
Herald of redemption story

DAFFODIL

Praise begets praise
   when our voices are raised.
Thoughts rising with the sun
   worship the Holy One.

Golden light rests warm upon
   everything the Creator made.
To feel him near and share delight
   is like a day without a night.

Lord, I love thee with all that I am,
   from feeble woman to little lamb.
I was designed to need and praise,
   like Daffodil cups respond to rays.

Bestow water, snow, dappled luster
   brilliant, gleaming, dazzling upward.
The scent is fresh and smells like green,
   smells like Eden yet to be seen.

Yellow opaque pleated petals,
   shaped as though sculpted of metal.
Nearby tangled tulip friends
   praise our Savior as they bend.

Proclaiming to those near and far
   joy birthed beneath brilliant star,
luminant life, lament, laughter
   and rising from death soon after.

CHILDREN

Fingerprints smeared on windows
Tiny, sweet little hands
Garbage on floor, garbage on wall
Tummies full, tummies small
Broken necklaces, smashed ornaments
Babies hugging adornments
Mismatched socks, purple boots
Boys and girls sharing shoes
Candy canes broken, sorry rarely spoken
Apologies come with mint kisses
Feet drag, bodies carried, legs kick
Or gallop gleefully, toes skip
Matted modest head of hair
Puffy chick without care
Comparisons, contrasts
Freedoms, forecast
Gifts or garbage
Rain or drink
War on the way we think

WALK

Orange, blue, red glass
Frosted lights from winters past
Strung to celebrate this year
The joy of life without fear

Green, yellow, purple glow
Stained glass in church window
Lighted patterns, baths of color
Welcome guests, create wonder

White, clear, crystal flakes
Flitter like fine-edged lace
White confetti crafted with care
Flutters down while we stare

Grey, translucent, smoky shadows
Fireplace coals, embers rattle
Source of warmth, sign of life
In the midst of winter's night

Cable-knit, red-'n-green mittens
Warm, wooly, soft as kittens
Hand-in-hand is how they fit
Tails of scarves flap in wind

Gold-'n-silver church bells chime
Shine, commemorate Christmas time
Musical melodies sung and heard
Proclaiming joy, peace to the world

TILES OF BEAUTY

Glimpse, spot
  beauty perceived
  day by day
  street by street.

Photos like patchwork
  form a quilt
  of color, light
  detail and fight.

Wrestling to perceive
  tiles to descry
  mundane personified
  glorified, exemplified.

A vast spread of intricacies
  natural and manmade
  pauses of pleasure
  moments of meander.

A sniff of the rose
  an alley adventure
  gazing at the sky
  staring at the trash.

Seeking Christ's face
  in patterns of rash
  in birth and decay
  in spring and fall.

In violets purple
   in seeds that swirl;
   garbage Thursday
   becomes paint Friday.

Muscle strains
   need rest, space
   to seek his face
   lest we forget.

PUDDLES

Puddles reflect, redirect surroundings.
When clear, we see the ground.
When bright, we see the sunlight,
the sky, the sun, the changing night.
When mixed, we see the muck,
brown-green-grey swirls stuck.
The mire settles, pond becomes clear.
An eye in the earth, we see our worth.
The dot of us against magnificent sky.
Why do we churn, disrupt and sigh.
The puddle now gone, evaporation.
Sight for a second, a revelation.
Insightful, yes; but grander still:
God who transform, restores and heals.

ICE

I am a block of ice
   brittle, crushed, cracked.
Perfect conditions
   keep me intact.
But to chip and melt
   is to reveal myself,
Just a puddle of water,
   needing drops of life.
Father, cup me
   when I'm falling,
As conditions change,
   shape and sculpt me.

TREES CLAP

The trees clap for our God.
    The wind blows by his power.
From the north, from the south
    the breeze eddies around me.

To the unseen, the King
    limbs first bend and bow.
Then shouts of *Hosanna!*
    I hear them now.

Their rustling turns quiet;
    trees know of Calvary.
They weep, they mourn;
    they supported our Savior.

He bleeds blood, then water;
    they seep sap that hardens.
The cross lay down, decayed;
    in a stone tomb he was laid.

We wait, all creation waits;
    then bursting forth on Easter morn,
Our Savior risen, the veil now torn!
    Fellowship, worship, forgiveness.

The trees resound with delight,
    claps of adoration, dappled light.
Songs of waving, no longer waiting;
    Christ has risen, a planter of seed.

LAYERS

Layers of beauty
Pastel sky
Dots of birds
Patterned flight
Cottonwood leaves
Dance with the breeze
Petals swirl, seeds scurry

Clouds form
Thunder rolls
Lightning awes
Rain provides
Rays penetrate
Dark sky
Sherbet sunset
Light lingers
Over grass and fingers

Comes stars
Shifting, moving
Art unfathomable
Wax rhetorical
Uncountable, shining up high

The moon follows
Its familiar trail
Perfect circle or thumbnail
Reaching high
Beyond our sphere
Creation in layers, our Maker appears

GALLERY

The sky daily exhibits your might,
    ever changing from dawn till night.
The vastness of color, the brilliance of light,
    moving, reassuring—a true delight.
The speck of me, the canvas of you;
    I am but a dot, a stroke or two.

Your masterful hand composes with care,
    billowing clouds and inserting air.
Truly, Father, you are an artist—
    from broad sweeping landscapes,
to the delicate details: boundless,
    limitless, infinite your works.

Watching and gazing, my knee jerks;
    fall down to ground; but music surrounds.
The greatness, grandeur of God abounds,
    evident through all his creation.
From the seed of the maple
    to the mountain foundations.

How, Lord, am I worthy to dwell in this
    masterpiece of sight, touch and smell?—
to fix my eyes on your unchanging mercies,
    to gape at the beauty unfurling before me.
Thank you, Lord, I can lie and stare
    at galleries of your work on earth, in air.

SNOWFLAKES

Joy floats like snowflakes dancing,
   soaring above buildings,
   sticking to trees at night,
   blanketing the landscape.

Glass stems, crystal leaves,
   mirrored, smiling sunrise
   shines on morning surprise;
   how could joy and I still meet?

Winter has lingered awhile
   subduing light, coating skin;
   happiness has no place in January
   with temporal pleasure thin.

But joy, peace, hope, Christ
   flutter by grace, flitter by love;
   breath of air, exhale the meek,
   whisper wonder worshipping.

Winds of heaven respire;
   fire kindled, spirit inflates;
   murmur a melodious hymn;
   by grace Shalom enters in.

Rising from darkness and cold,
   nestle with Northern Lights.

PAINTING OF WHITE

Water colors—an art of painting with sight:

Planning ahead, holding the white,
    protecting its place, holding its lines.

Water so important makes art alive with
    puddling colors, sprays and surprise.

Pooling in places, lie for awhile, then
    dry like snowflakes with crystal smiles.

Mistakes dabbed with cotton, patience needed;
    blending intended at times or separations beading.

Father, your skilled hands use Living Water, paint
    with masterful strokes heavy, fine or faint.

Waiting for beauty to unfold, future chapters to be told;
    all works together; colors unseen, colors new.

Crimson strokes; royal blue the Son's beauty,
    spear-pierced side's sudden flow of blood and water.

Masterpiece of white.

HUNT

Hunt for treasure,
for beauty, for pleasure.

Think of what's lovely and pure;
search the sidewalk curbs.

Grey skies, grey ground,
not much to be found.

Then I spot a green dot,
a bud of life, spring caught.

Continue on the weathered path;
sift through garbage and trash.

Doors of copper shed their skin;
knobs of mint blend in.

Bicycles locked to trees and fence;
wheels of color, shadows dispense.

Symbols carved in limestone
ages, years, attached to homes.

Brown trees and limbs empty
but filled with robins a-plenty.

Roots of a tree knobbed and twisted,
lying on each other, they whisper.

Bark rough, brown and wet,
moss of chartreuse, orange sunset.

Grape vines twisted around a post,
shriveled berries, dotted coast.

Metal hub caps layered with snows
mirror the white, tiny windows.

Think of such things.—
Find them, rejoice!

Beauty laced in unlikely places;
one of our Lord's several graces.

STAINED GLASS

Glory in pieces
Light divided
Colorful scenes
Truth confided

Loveliness lies
On floors, on doors
On skin, on hats
On the sick and sore

For minutes each day
The colorful display
Soul lifted
Savior gifted

Bones broken
Body shattered
Faithful in desert
Friends scatter

Christ on cross
Split by our cost
Arise beauty, arise Son
Fill the dark, O Promised One

Stained-glass work of art
Splendid, radiant, healed heart

BUBBLING BROOK

As life-giving water trickles downstream,
   the source is a bit hidden it would seem.
Quickly the water rushes and rises
   in bubbles frothy and whipped, like cream.

Now conquering rocks, the water persists
   around them, over the powerful fists.
Strength serene and sweetly flowing,
   a river coursing its way, not slowing.

Creeks of joy feed into the whole,
   make the path wide and full.
Leaves mingle, downward sailing
   to lower ground, winds prevailing.

Where waters are still and grasses are soft,
   the river dances over the hills.
The bubbling brook changes course,
   revealing its providential purpose.

A place of repose, a place of rest.
   Come, Lord Jesus, be my guest.
In these gentle waters we meet;
   with one look I'm known, intimate.

My goals, my thoughts and all my failings,
   a heart of meekness seeking my Savior.
Deep calls to deep, in my eyes you peek,
   knowing what's behind and what lies before.
You beckon me to drink from the waters once more.

CHRIST

*But I pray to you, Lord,
in the time of your favor;
in your great love, O God,
answer me with your sure salvation.*

–Psalm 69:13

SIGHT

No eye has seen, no ear has heard
the reward for those who trust the Word.

Brightness shining like the sun
Color of springtime in flower buds
The ripple of wind against the water
Arms that hold us, our Heavenly Father
Skin soft as peach, stars we cannot reach
Chartreuse moss, cyan sky
Magenta sunsets in velvet nights
Emerald streets, ruby roads
Foundations of pearl and rose
Towering cities, shadows gone
Rainbow harmony, a hue song
Painted canvases, pointed steeples
Balance of beauty by those who were feeble

Living with us, a King with no throne
Whose marvel cannot be etched in stone
His glory dwelling and yet reaching
Beyond the heights, leaving us speechless
Bend low, lie before
The Sight that makes our eyes sore
Knees upon jewels, toes on clouds

'Holy, holy,' we yell aloud.

HEAR

Chiming bells, we wish you well
Strings plucked, melody stuck on refrain
Strum, drum, pick the cello
Music loud, strains mellow
Up and down the tempo goes
Angel choruses we do not know
Sounds so sweet they draw a tear

At intermission the notes disappear
Why is there a break in the music?
Is there ever a waiting on sonnets?

Sounds so lovely, echoes reverberate
Instruments tuned, organs calibrated
Go, stop, go; pauses in perfection
Angel legions playing percussion
Thousands upon thousands singing a song
The mighty and meek joining the throng
With multitudes of heavenly beings
Shouting praises and joyfully singing

Flocks of followers gathering for the feast
The Lamb's voice pleasantly rings
His blood raised in a toast
Glasses tink, plink, and boast
Melodies merry, cadence, chorus
flowing sound, metered focus

And if we had one-thousand ears,
the beauty would linger endless years.

TASTE

Sips of soda, sugar suds
Sprinkles on a cupcake
Taste buds delight, awake
Peppermint, red and white
(Stripes of our Savior's might)
Tart lemon, juicy tang
Carrots munching
A chorus sang
Symphony of senses

Glimpses of grace
Pointing to a loftier place
Revealing, satisfying, securing faith
Upward, onward yet we yearn
To God's promises in turn
Due time, green tomato on vine
Months ahead, watermelon bed
Nectar dripping from summer bees
Acorns stored in winter trees
Seasons of waiting
Then comes celebrating

SCENT

Born in a barn of cows,
    scents linger: manure,
    wet hay, rotting wood;
    a birth not understood.

Dust-filled nostrils
    during desert perils
    need quenching water
    to soothe dried skin.

Wilderness wandering,
    locust's lament,
    all his energy spent:
    tempter's reasons for bread.

Stones our Savior chooses instead;
    dry earth, little worth,
    eyes too baked to tear,
    sores with arid blood smears.

Then the smell of fish and friendship
    followed by pharisee resentment;
    rich wine the scent to come
    after the bitter deed is done.

Perfumed hair smelling sweet
    pales against disciples feet.
    Bread this time the Lord accepts,
    but soon we all will forget.

Olive trees' mingled leaves
    shuffle in the nighttime breeze;
    snores of brothers, sour breath,
    prayers of pain, night without rest.

The stench of betrayal,
    the foulness at hand,
    accusations, bitter demands,
    condemnation's curses.

A washing of hands,
    a march to the hill
    where bones rot, blood spills;
    decay driven into his feet.

All is quiet; mother's care provided,
    veil torn, women mourn,
    frankincense and myrrh—
    now a different kind of present.

Burial cloths, damp cave;
    all our filth he forgave.
    Stench of defeat was predicted;
    instead, he rose in victory!

Lilies white, daffodil bulbs,
    tulip trees, hyacinth calls;
    scents so pure, so lovely and mild
    adorn the head of a faithful Child.

Crown of thorns crushed,
    weeds pulled, field threshed;
    sweet harvest of saints.
    My soul faints.

TOUCH

The rugged cross we touch
We cringe
Splinters enter in
Roughness, rawness, decay and rust
This was ours had the Son not trusted
Submitted himself to his father's hands
Inscribed by the eternal I Am

Letters long as miles
Names upon name piles
Scratched, scraped the spotless Lamb
Father like Son, covered in brands
Blood-covered prints
Scab-crusted sores
Touch reduced by searing thorns
Seeping scratches
Brittle bones
Pierced by a sword
Tossed at with stones

Risen in glory!
Our hands raise high
Healing and beauty
No spear in the side
Smoothness like oil
Softness like fleece
Fingers open in release and praise
Feathered future
Pardoned past
Silk garments that will last

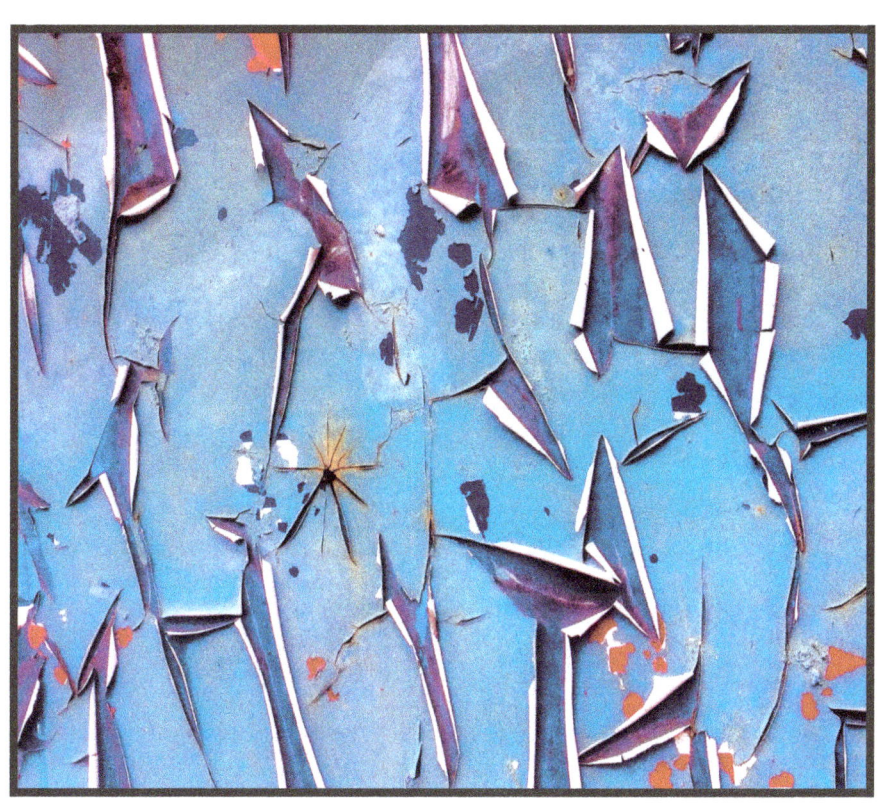

FALL

Fall the season
Fall down steps
Fall of man, a truth we accept

Thorns in gardens
Thorns in backs
Thorns choke when I lack

Cast out of Eden
Faces downcast
Future of gray, a negative forecast

A rescue plan
For the planet of man
Far beyond what we understand

A babe for a King
A cross we now sing
Eternal life bought by suffering

Needles of pain
Needles of thorns
Muscles ache and muscles torn

We wait in hope
We wait for the day
When our Savior washes the gray

Light shines bright
No black, but white
Midnight sparkles, suffering subsides

The thought of whole
Of toil no more
Of a body restored by nail and sword

Forever spring
Forever we sing
Eternal symphonies, no more sympathies

Vision of healing
Vision of might
Vision of darkness, a fleeting kite

Mercy in morning
Mourning no more
Joyful meetings, fellowship restored

Exodus, now entry
Cacophony, now harmony
Martyrs become brothers, sisters turn saints

The old is gone
The new has come
Fall is no more, because of the Son

WEIGHT OF GLORY

O weight of glory,
  my soul knows the story.
Rise up again and hope, my friend.
  My 'lack of worth,' it isn't true,
nor the blue, gray state of mind.
  Turn me forward, not behind.

A fresh breeze settles in.
  Lungs absorb the oxygen.
Breathe in me your life-giving Word.
  Let it settle, refresh me, Lord.
Lies are like weights we carry,
  dumbbells weighting neck and knee.
Crumbling, crushing, catastrophes:
  do we need to carry these?
Are they real or imagined?
  Help me sift through to truth.
Let your Word be my sieve.
  Let it filter, faithful Friend:
goodness, trustworthiness and kindness,
  holiness, joy, delight and sight.

Jesus broke the chains in my name;
  now no further condemnation.
You descended to depths of dread
  and rose to high bouquets of beauty.
Pain and suffering I know about,
  not destruction, desolation, doubt.
Fathom I cannot, what was done
  in my place on and after the cross.

GIFT

The kingdom of God is a gift
  not achieved by a list
  without merit or claim
  received by the helpless
  life for the lifeless
  gates opened wide
  no patrons inside

Only the meek and meager,
  the humble believers
  who take Christ at his Word
  (the Word become Flesh
  that breathed and died)
  will be triumphantly freed

Who broke the chains of hell
  to restore, cleanse, save us
  so that we might praise him
  we might pass on the gift
  that's been given

We can celebrate with the lost
  we can talk about his cost
  and our gain
  A gift

SABBATICAL BREAK

Father, how specifically you answer prayer:
   Laughter in our home, children growing strong
   Health to dance, occasionally leap
   Eyes mostly dry, hardly ever weep
   Flowers grow abundantly
   Friends celebrate joyfully

Husband and I hold hands, make plans
   Greet neighbors, meet new couples
   We pray, eat, juggle
   Receive children's bedtime kisses
   They've witnessed your goodness
   We rest, remember, write

May our praise be more than at night
   When I rise to your light
   Cloaked with the sun's rays
   Let me worship you in delight
   You are my God, to you I pray

Midday may I seek your counsel
   Help me to be still and listen
   Resting by your streams of glass
   Waiting in the greening grass
   There I see you pass

Father, at bedtime may I recall this
   Sabbatical break, prayers tall
   May I sleep in peace
   Your angels guard us
   Dreaming of beauty and rest

REMEMBER

Tears rush down my face
Mercy's waves absorb
Grace anchors my form
Toppled over, but straining
My face above, proclaiming

Goodness glitters by your light
Darkness flees at your sight
The water deep, a mystery
My anchor secure indefinitely
The Rock of Ages, the true Foundation
The Lion of Judah, my faithful Fortress

I stare at the horizon
I look up
Clouds of peace envelop
with pardon, perfection, piety
Jesus, God Incarnate, deity
Fears, pain, strain I recall
Suffering, strife, turmoil
Hopes dim, my body thin
Lying in this place
I remember grace

FOCUS

Like a lighthouse
You guide me to your haven
Praise my God, sing with me
Shout accolades, voice serenades
The good Father guides us home
The pilgrimage long
The passengers strong
Stand beside me
Carry my burdens, lift me up

Praise be to Jesus, his Body and Cup
Praise to the Spirit, enduring, holding secure
Praise to the Father, our Living Water
Who, seeing and knowing me
He loves me freely

Let your presence wash over me
Dwell in my flesh
Flood me with thanksgiving
For I am forgiven
Soak me in your holy scriptures
Let me hear your whisper
Like the morning dew
Let me see your mercies anew

PREPARATION

Preparation, then feast:
  silver cleaned, name cards placed.
Tables set, casseroles cooked,
  eager faces in a room.

Lord, you're preparing me
  for celebrations yet unseen.
Joshua roamed the desert awhile
  to learn from Moses, to be a child.

Joseph served as a slave;
  wisdom over time he gave.
Star-filled skies, promises in sand
  prepared the man Abraham.

Waiting, working, worshiping,
  tested and tried; God would provide.
Teaching Ten Commandments,
  triune God, Father and Son.

Desert wanderings: all for naught?;
  suffering while being taught.
Preparing forty days and nights,
  part of promises having sight.

Careful craft of hulking ark;
  Noah saved, animals marched.
Preparation of a burial space;
  the Lord arose in that place.

Paths laid by saints of old
  retell the story long foretold.
That day when we feast with our Lord,
  preparation will be done.

Will we eat casseroles, perhaps?

HOLY ONE

Holy, radiant One,
beautiful, infinite;
  a sight for sore eyes,
  you bring souls flight.

Edges glow,
leaves illuminated;
  the sun rises, golden butter
  melting on the horizon.

Sweetness flows effortless,
brilliance manifest;
  churning from one day
  to the next.

A path or perfect arch,
trail drawn in detail;
  warmth, delight, sight,
  daytime songs before night.

Sun low in cloud shows
amber, fuchsia, plum;
  it slides beneath hills,
  and all seems still.

Its glory refracts,
our thoughts distract;
  the sun, spoken Word,
  a poetry of pleasure.

Ordained by the Father,
upheld by the Son;
  homonyms meet, greet,
  bring us to our knees.

Glory unconfined,
splendor shouting;
  burst, blast, blaze,
  surge, spill, spout.

Unveiled majesty,
in wonder worshiping.

RIGHT NOW

Right now I seek you, Father:
   the brilliance of your face,
   truth in this place.

Right now I reflect on the grave:
   Saturday the day in between,
   mourning before morning.

Right now I remember the Cross:
   the crown of rose thorns,
   the red drops, the scorn.

Right now I long for the eternal:
   to sing the triumph song,
   to shout accolades, fear gone.

Easter Eve, no preparations made:
   Sabbath, the Father bids us rest;
   the Son defeats, while we nest.

Eggshells crack, crumble, new life:
   out of darkness and hardness,
   baby birds sing with gladness.

We and all creation wait:
   hoping and remembering,
   then tomorrow we celebrate.

KING

Christ the King
Angels sing
Multitudes in the sky
Glory personified
Humble manger
Always in danger
Threatened by kings
A serpent who sings
Satan chanting
Lies sweet as pie
A trap too small
The devil will fall
Messiah prophesies
Ascension to the skies
Seated on the Throne
The Judge of his own
He, the Firstborn Heir
We, descendants by prayer
Gold, myrrh, frankincense
Grace our recompense

MERCY

How do we praise you, Lord,
when your mercy is great,
your compassion evident,
and your love everlasting?

When cancer is removed,
when the body is healed,
when a scan comes back clear,
how do we begin?

I cry. You hear us, Lord, you
who are near the brokenhearted.
You restore the sick.
They fly on wings of butterflies.

We rejoice, Father, overwhelmed.
How do I praise you, Holy One,
Comforter, King?—Just thank you, Lord.
Thank you for a friend restored.

BOW

Why do we not bow?
Have we now forgotten our place?
Nose to dirt, knees collapsed,
arms outspread, eyes spilling;
from dirt we're made and will return.

I lie me down in this place
to humble myself before you now;
bend me like a flat bow.
Make me supple and flexible
for the work you've given me.

Bind me from one end to the other,
to walk in truth on a narrow path.
Would the words that come be arrows
to pierce my heart and those of others.
I am yours, Lord; carry me.

In your hands I can do anything.
Break my pride, warp my selfishness.
Sand my roughness, notch my needs.
My back arches, face to ground;
bent, warped, shaped from earth.

Lord, angels bow before you.
All creation hangs on your words.
We are but flowers in a field:
bending, nodding, breathing, dying.
Bow to the one with keys of life.

Help me not forget who I serve:
loving Father, mighty King,
Jesus Messiah, flames of fire,
feet of brass, blazing brightness,
emanating glory that lasts.

Alpha, Omega who roars like waters;
He's alive forevermore.
Kneel before the holy one.
Bow to our Maker, Master Craftsman,
who ends all war, restores
the pure in heart.

TO BE A BABY

To be a baby
To rest in a lap
To suckle milk
To laugh
To be carried
To be loved
To be kissed
To be hugged
To be cradled
and caressed;
Father, thank you;
I am blessed.

FIX MY EYES

Lord, help me fix my eyes
  on the ribbon of revelations.
Help me continue to run
  in the midst of pain and tribulations.
Breathe in and out of this earthly tent.
Patch my holes, anchor my post.
Shield me from onslaught of rain,
  fear, guilt, worry; a soul slain.
Smile on me, Lord; show your favor
  to this jar of clay that's tipped over.
With your hand mend my cracks.
Paint me with thanks. May I spill over.
The treasure of your Spirit guarded by frailty,
  like the ark of the covenant covered in wood.
How can the holy rest in the broken?
How can you reside there and glorify?
I am nothing, have nothing apart from you;
  fix my mind on this truth.
May I run when my shoes are worn,
  when my muscles ache and are torn,
  when clothes cling, when the trail fades,
  when fog festers, and faint is the horn.
As darkness settles and my lamp flickers,
  the only oil remaining is on my head;
  rise within me, precious treasure, Guarantee.
Give rhythm to my steps and air in my lungs.
Guard my feet from stumbling
  till they stand before you.
No more groans, no more grumbling,
  only praise-filled shouts and peaceful sighs,
  eyes fixed on my Messiah, my prize.

SACRIFICE

The more we comprehend sacrifice,
  the more we see love.
Just a petal, a spray of perfume.
Would a wedding bring tears
  had the father not given the bride?

What about the mother bird
  who shelters with her side.
The pounding, the cold, the suffering;
  love not understood, but we sing.

Offering of comfort
Offering for sin
Offering of life
Offering of kin
Gifts, surrender, love
Father's Son instead of dove
Hung upon the cross
Dead for our dross
Tears for years
The Father's loss
Victory
The ultimate cost
Lovingly given
Patiently taught
The sacrifice of love
Holiness not forgot
Revealed through hardship
Requires our worship
Unveiling, unearthing
Sacrifice bringing light to love

WONDER

*When I consider your heavens,
the work of your fingers,
the moon and the stars,
which you have set in place,
what is mankind that you are mindful of them,
human beings that you care for them?*

–Psalm 8:3-4

CAPTURED

My heart is captured and claimed,
   devoted to Christ's name.
Day and night he is my delight,
   the only thing I desire to write.

Praise to God, who made me,
   formed me, trained me.
He has gathered me as his child
   for Paradise. I smile.

What peace is there other than God,
   whose promises flow faithfully.
The ocean filled with his love would
   be mere drops from above.

His presence, his friendship and face
   is what I seek, what I crave.

FULLY KNOWN

Fully known, fully loved,
grace upon grace,
white as a dove;
the all-seeing eye
of my Lord loved me
in bounty and storm.
He seeks the lost,
calls me by name.
Beloved am I;
that will not change.
He pries my heart,
just like a clam,
open to the great I Am.
Despite my dross,
he sees whiteness.
The pearl of Christ,
my precious treasure
buried inside
my weathered shell,
shines bright,
a light on a hilltop.
Now I proclaim
this love nonstop;
shout it, scream it
with all of my voice,
a thing of beauty, a
musical noise;
fully known, protected, loved.

All the gems of the sea
can't compare to Christ in me.

HEAVEN'S GATE

Through Heaven's Gate I enter in,
  walls of pearl covered in vines.
Angel trumpets vibrate the ground,
  toes tapping in gate behind.
Trees of fruit ever bearing,
  of sweetness beyond comparing.
Animals chase just for sport
  in light so bright my eyes are sore.
Walking on, I journey deeper
  to see my Father and my Keeper.
I hear his voice; I begin to jog.
  'Lord, was that you in the fog?'
Beams of brilliance penetrate;
  the clouds of earth I have escaped.
I fall down before Son of Man,
  my knees sinking in the sand.
Jesus Christ, right of the Throne,
  beckons I stand. 'Welcome home!'
We embrace. I—an heir!—
  take my place. He pulls up a chair.
I sit to a feast that dazzles and fills,
  because my Savior's blood was spilled.
He who bought me at enormous cost
  calls me upward—no longer lost.

WHEN THE MOON RISES

When the moon rises
  I wrestle in bed,
tossing and turning,
  a baby bird unfed.

Chirping, I talk and squawk
  squeal, sulk in thought;
waiting in pain, wanting
  to escape, see daybreak.

My feathered friends
  sleep in their beds,
no battle of words, but
  peaceful foreheads.

When the moon rises
  I talk to you, Father.
Because you care deeply,
  we spend hours together.

Lord, I know you better,
  realize my place and need,
like a chick in her nest,
  who must wait patiently.

Your wings cover the clouds,
  the owl that haunts my sight.
I find refuge in your arms—
  promising light, not harm.

BREAKTHROUGH

In the chess game behind the scenes, Lord,
    help me wait for the game, set, match,
    help me be a tool in your mighty sack.
I pray for a breakthrough for those I love,
    for those who are stalled,
    for my own heart.
Lord you rejected gall, accepted each ounce of pain;
    sin's crushing weight
    rested upon
    a small sip of vinegar.
You refused, your senses alert, not confused,
    and broke through the veil
    torn from the top.
The sky darkened, sun stopped, you broke through
    the shadows of Sheol,
    redeemed the lost,
    rescued my soul.
In comparison, how microscopic my requests seem.
    Guard me from the evil one.
    Set my heart on things above.
    Rest me in unfailing love.
May I witness victory in how people see,
    needs met, hopes fed,
    soup for dinner, a side of bread,
    the gospel proclaimed.
All in Christ's holy name.

ROSE AND THORN

Trail of a rose,
   roots and earth,
   growth; but then
   thorns surface.

Road of ridicule,
   lies prick,
   serpent slithers,
   slander spits.

Twisted, tangled,
   needing trimmed;
   shears prune,
   hand guides.

Plant sees light,
   receives life,
   rising above
   thorn and muck.

Rosebud reveals
   what was stuck;
   beauty unfurling,
   sweet scents whirling.

Grace abounding,
   colors surrounding
   red red rose;
   blood drips to nose.

My Savior mild,
   a humble child;
   now ring of thorns.
   Mary mourns.

Savior, when we meet,
   may my fragrance be
   the aroma of my Lord,
   rose scent in the thorn.

HUMBLED

Too humble to write,
I ponder this gift
to see you in your glory
and write pieces of the story.

A truth woven through time
of a love pure, sublime.
Tear drops, crystals on my face
refract your majesty in this place.

Baffled that you would use
a farmer's daughter, I muse
how blessings upon blessings flow
down to us on this Earth below.

Someday I will see your fountain
bubbling, brimming, singing,
worshiping Creator King
mindful of me. Can this be?

Babe in manger, humblest of all;
mother beside, nursing in straw;
father bends low, burden on back.
Shepherds kneel; in the light they bask.

The humble One received gifts of gold
that paled in the luster of three nails.
Resurrection, remembrance, jubilance.
Humbly I'll write with this gift of sight.

SEEDLING

Mustard seed small and round,
   planted in fertile ground,
covered in soil, splashed in rain,
   sprout of life, Victor's gain.

Protector from choking thorns,
   guardian of fire and smoke.
Caretaker of the land,
   support me as I stand.

Taller I grow, awkward at first.
   Bearing fruit, I now thirst.
Roots wiggle down
   through rock and mound.

Leaching fuel, food and faith;
   sweet Savior full of grace,
uphold me through the seasons
   when drought threatens reason.

When tread upon by wild beast,
   when fowl swoops to steal the yeast,
when days are long and nights linger,
   when spikes penetrate my fingers.

At the appointed harvest time,
   yielding its bounty and its wine,
friends will gather, amazed
   at the blessing of this place.

Stories will be told of a seedling small,
who was strengthened by a God most tall.

ABOUT THE POET

Sarah Suzanne Noble grew up on a farm in Indiana. She graduated with her Masters in Architecture from Ball State University in 2008. She practiced architecture and design for several years.

The poems in this book, her first volume of poetry, were inspired by Ann Voskamp's *1000 Gifts*, Timothy Keller's *Reflections on the Psalms*, and the daily devotions of Oswald Chambers. In all three sources, Sarah has found endless support.

Sarah and her husband, Jonny, attend Park Community Church in Chicago, Illinois, where they serve as deacons. They are involved in several ministries, including marriage mentoring and crisis support. The Nobles have two children, Ruthie and Jacob.

Find Sarah online at:
    her Website: www.sarahsuzannenoble.com
    her Instagram page: #Sarahsuzannenoble

www.ingramcontent.com/pod-product-compliance
Lightning Source LLC
Chambersburg PA
CBHW050016090426
42734CB00021B/3288